My P Words

Consultants

Ashley Bishop, Ed.D.
Sue Bishop, M.E.D.

Publishing Credits

Dona Herweck Rice, *Editor-in-Chief*
Robin Erickson, *Production Director*
Lee Aucoin, *Creative Director*
Sharon Coan, *Project Manager*
Jamey Acosta, *Editor*
Rachelle Cracchiolo, M.A.Ed., *Publisher*

Image Credits
All Shutterstock images.

Teacher Created Materials
5301 Oceanus Drive
Huntington Beach, CA 92649-1030
http://www.tcmpub.com
ISBN 978-1-4333-2557-1
© 2012 Teacher Created Materials, Inc.
Printed in China 51497

I see a pig.

I see a **p**izza.

I see a **p**ie.

I see a **p**arrot.

I see a **p**iano.

I see a **p**umpkin.

I see a panda.

I see a parachute.

I see a park.

Glossary

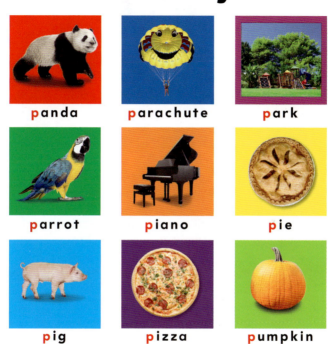

panda   parachute   park

parrot   piano   pie

pig   pizza   pumpkin

Sight Words

I   see   a

Activities

- Read the book aloud to your child, pointing to the *p* words as you say them. After reading each page, ask, "What do you see?"

- Find a recipe to make pumpkin pie and make one with your child. Or, buy a frozen one to bake and share. Remind your child that the words *pumpkin* and *pie* begin with *p*.

- Go to the park with your child. Ask your child what is his or her favorite thing to do at the park.

- Find pictures of parrots from the Internet or from books at the library and have your child choose one to draw or paint a picture of.

- Help your child think of a personally valuable word to represent the letter *p*, such as *pet*.